WE ARE
VICTIMS
—OF OUR—
THOUGHTS

Discover The Power That Influences Your
Decision Making

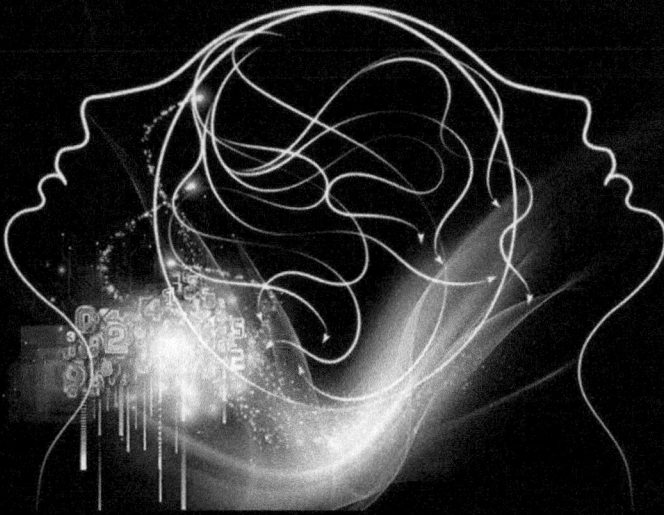

Eddy & Kareen L. Nelson

We Are Victims Of Our Thoughts
Copyright © 2023 by Eddy and Kareen L. Nelson

Editor: Barracks Editorial & Design House, LLC. @ iambevtheeditor@gmail.com

Book Cover: Designby_nazia @ www.fiverr.com

Back Photos: Simplephoto1014@gmail - Isaiah Nelson

All Scripture quotations marked (NLT) are taken from the Holy Bible, New Living Translation, copyright ©1996, 2004, 2015 by Tyndale House Foundation. Used by permission of Tyndale House Publishers, Carol Stream, Illinois 60188. All rights reserved.

Scripture quotations marked KJV are taken from *The Holy Bible* KJV, Cambridge Edition: 1769; King James Version Bible Online, 2015. http://www.kingjamesbible.org. Used by permission. All rights reserved.

Scripture quotations noted (NIV) are taken from The Holy Bible, New International Version (NIV) Copyright 1973, 1978, 1984, 2011, by Biblica, Inc. Used by permission. All rights reserved worldwide.

ISBN: 979-8-218-14438-8

Printed in the United States of America

WE ARE VICTIMS

OF

OUR THOUGHTS

Discover the Power that Influences your Decision Making

GIFTED TO:

_____

FROM:

_____

ENDORSEMENT

"My daughter and son-in-love shared a revelatory, engaging collaboration exploring choice and deception with us.

Likewise, my late wife, Gloria, would agree we must commit to transforming our thought lives." An Excellent read.

Rev. Dr. Prince Coke, Th.D.
Senior Pastor
Outreach Baptist Church
Bronx, New York

DEDICATION

This book is dedicated to anyone who has ever felt like the Victim of their thoughts.

CONTENTS

INTRODUCTION

～

After a busy week, a lazy Sunday afternoon in sunny South Florida was precisely what the doctor ordered.

On this Sunday in December, my husband and I decided to spend the day at home relaxing. Over the past two years, we have been living with the Covid 19 *pandemic*, grieving the loss of those we loved and feeling the loss of those we didn't know. The world was rapidly changing whether we understood the cause or wanted to change with it. Thankfully, we have faith in God and have grown through life-changing experiences, so we have remained focused during this new period of change caused by Covid 19.

So, as my husband and I was having lunch and engaged in conversation, he suddenly shocked me by admitting he was "tired of being a victim of his thoughts."

When I heard that, my first reaction was to ask, "Where did that come from"?

My mind wondered if this was the result of prolonged pandemic frustration.

According to his heartfelt words, he described this discovery as a revelation and expressed frustration over its discovery, which he said: "should have been obvious before."

His words immediately made me think, "Wow, what a great title for a book!"

After he explained some of his experiences and the one that sparked the idea we will discuss later, it became evident that we would collaborate on a book together.

Our aim is to unravel this to shed light on the aspects of ourselves that are shaped by our thoughts and to understand whether we are indeed victims.

Our lives are a series of thoughts that shape who we are and what we can become.

When a thought occurs, the mind decides if that idea is worth pursuing because our brain controls our thoughts through our acceptance. Similarly, a red traffic light at an intersection causes the mind to react automatically by waiting for it to turn green.

The same should apply to our thoughts, beliefs, and behaviors, and we are to carefully consider them before committing ourselves.

Do we fall victim to deception, or do we fail to distinguish between truth and lies?

Think about the times when you were wrong about the thoughts you acted on. Unfortunately, there may have been times when our thoughts led us into a situation we shouldn't have been in.

Do you remember that time or incidents when you overruled caution? Only after you put things into proper perspective did you ask yourself how you became involved in that mess. It is important not to obsess over it, but you must take responsibility for your thoughts contributing to your situation.

Imagine that your thoughts function like a time clock. It is happening whether we are aware of it or not. It is impossible to stop the constant flow of information in our heads. Every aspect of our lives is influenced by how we communicate, what we wear, eat, and socialize.

Our minds are flooded with ideas we cannot wait to act upon. So we breathe life into our thoughts to act on what is in our hearts. That said, you decide what happens to your thoughts regardless of your intentions or what has influenced them.

In this context, a victim is someone who has been deceived or tricked in some way despite being innocent. We will explore what a Victim Of Our Thoughts means from an objective, biblical, and social angle.

To claim that **We Are Victims Of Our Thoughts**, we must acknowledge our innocence and supply adequate evidence proving it. We must put our opinions and viewpoints aside to analyze our thoughts objectively. There is so much to understand about yourself through your thought patterns.

We will also identify who influences our thinking. Finally, you will learn how to refine your thinking to make better decisions. As we unravel this, you may think we are the victims. You might think there is a victim mentality behind the deception.

When you consider yourself a victim of the negative actions of others, and you behave based on these beliefs, you may think the deception is us as the victim.

After reading this book, you can make an informed decision. Our plan is for you to assess your position in life by evaluating your thoughts and understanding whether you need to change the **trajectory** of your thinking.

As you learn about the power of your thoughts, you can decide whether you are innocent or guilty based on personal decisions and what is true.

1

THOUGHTS ARE POWERFUL

A thought is the most incredible first source of power humanity has. In simplest terms, a thought is an idea, suggestion, or memory produced by thinking that usually occurs suddenly in the mind. Whenever your mind can conceive something, a thought introduces it.

Our thoughts carry great weight and significance, which is why they are essential. Why? Because you breathe life into your desires through your thoughts.

Thoughts are strong, so it is not easy to stop thinking about what you are thinking. However, by trying not to think about them, you will think more about them, which is why thoughts can be so powerful.

Do you have trouble falling asleep at night because you can't shut down your mind?

Likewise, it is common for our thoughts to make us feel like a victim throughout the day.

Have you ever wondered why you can't just let go and end those thoughts so you can move on with your life?

How easy should it be to move negative thoughts out of your consciousness? Unfortunately, it's not that easy!

In some cases, emotional issues are deep and do not surface often. However, those issues require you to be vulnerable and honest to resolve them.

There may be uncertainty about the present, even fear about the future, or an uneasy feeling about your past decisions. However, you will discover your authentic self as you examine the path of negative thoughts while being open to your emotions and fears.

In Genesis chapter one, let us look at how God created the earth through the power of His thoughts.

Through an idea, a thought produced God's spoken Word to form the earth. God thought, visualized it, then said, "let there be light," "let there be seas," "let there be the heavens," and so on that was created.

Similarly, we can think simultaneously while visualizing what we want and create it with the action from our thoughts.

We can speak life into a dead situation, create, encourage, and bring about joy as God did through His thoughts.

However, our thoughts can create an undesirable environment by devaluing ourselves and others with the actions of our thoughts.

Nothing is greater than God's thoughts and power, and He wants to share it with you to a greater degree. This ability is already within us, but the real power to demonstrate lies with us by transforming and renewing our minds through Christ Jesus.

Through humility and faith in God, those who believe in Jesus' redemptive power can operate supernaturally to rule over evil.

The ability to command and gain access is given to you when you are born again. No, it is not about physical birth but receiving a spiritual renewal. We are born in a corrupted state by inheritance since the original sin in the garden by Adam and Eve.

Our souls must be reborn, regenerated from above, pure, and righteous again the way God created us to be.

In addition to not having to be performance-based or achieved by religious ceremonies or traditional rites, the new birth illustrates God's Spirit.

The Bible states that God is not a respecter of persons; it is a personal choice that everyone can receive. It has already been provided, but God gave us free will to accept it.

You reconnect with your supernatural spiritual nature by accepting Jesus as your Lord and Savior today. It is a realm beyond the natural that cannot be seen or touched, giving you access to a new domain of power.

If you do not realize your divine status, you will operate and get results according to your human nature, not by the Spirit of God.

As a spiritual being, your new birth makes you a spirit operating in a body. Therefore, your future will depend on understanding your unique and new nature revealed in God's Word.

Studying God's Word will constantly develop your faith. The stronger your belief, the more powerful your command level will be.

A deeper relationship with our Creator gives us authority, dominion, ideas, and creativity through the God aspect unfolding through our thoughts. Your relationship with Christ will guide you towards a stronger faith and your identity in Him.

It is the law of life that everything produces after its own kind. Therefore, you will reap good results if you engage in good thoughts, but thinking of evil thoughts to gain good results is detrimental.

It is written in Galatians 6:7, "Be not deceived; God is not mocked: for whatsoever a man soweth, that shall he also reap."

We are what we think and what we put into our minds. This concept is so powerful that if you think you are rich, you can *very well* become rich.

It is impossible to become wealthy if you believe you are poor.

Everything results from an individual's thoughts, whether good or bad. Your thoughts drive your actions, but it is in your heart that gives life to that idea.

Think of your thoughts as a vehicle moving too fast out of control; you must slow down and apply the brakes to stop it. For example, you meet someone you like and plan how this will work out. Your plan for how this will work out is based on the person you met and how you think they are.

However, you acted too quickly based on your thoughts, and the relationship ended after two months. Why the person did not present the truth or what you thought they would be.

Moving too fast without considering all the possible outcomes without the correct information is dangerous. But, unfortunately, thinking this way is also how we become victims of our thoughts.

Our thoughts can also be redirected if they are heading in the wrong direction because we control them.

The following examples will illustrate my point.

When you begin to think of drinking, you become a drinker, which can lead to you becoming an alcoholic. It's time to refocus your thinking on why you are an alcoholic with a changed mindset and another productive activity.

Smoking harms your health, and considering you were warned about it but ignored it, you should do something about how you think about it. Focus your energies on resources that will assist you in quitting.

Losing weight is not about how you think about it but how you plan to lose weight. Redirecting your efforts to lose weight by changing your lifestyle is a good idea.

We are in a power struggle; whether we are victorious or defeated, believers or non-believers depends on our thought process. Therefore, taking our thoughts seriously and directing them aptly is crucial.

We prefer a victim mentality since we are not fully aware of the consequences of our decisions and actions. Therefore, it does not matter whether we agree with an idea but say we are still ignorant of its outcome concerning that idea.

We justify our innocence when we choose to accept or reject something. However, we will be in unpleasant situations if we do not control our thoughts.

It is not only immoral thoughts that are bad, but those that keep us from our Savior or make us stuck in our emotions and feelings.

You live through your emotions and feelings when you fight for fame, fortune, or material things for selfish reasons.

If your thoughts are consumed by gratifying those needs, you might be willing to give up your soul. Your thoughts will cause you to act wrongly if you don't control your heartbreak and anger.

Many people have experienced trauma that has left them victims of their own thoughts.

For instance, I was trapped in an elevator as a child for about 30 minutes, which made me afraid of elevators for many years. Finally, almost twenty years later, it was time to admit that my fear was real and that the only way to overcome it was through a change in my mindset.

The spiritual battle we fight is in our minds. Therefore, the only way to select the right thoughts God initiates is when we recognize the presence of God as our thoughts.

God wants us to make the right choices and helps us by giving us good thoughts. These scriptures will say it better.

2 Corinthians 10:3-5 "For though we walk in the flesh, we do not war after the flesh: (For the weapons of our warfare are not carnal, but mighty through God to the pulling down of strong holds;) Casting down imaginations, and every high thing that exalteth itself against the knowledge of God, and bringing into captivity every thought to the obedience of Christ." And

Philippians 4:8 "Finally, brethren, whatsoever things are true, whatsoever things are honest, whatsoever things are just, whatsoever things are pure, whatsoever things are lovely, whatsoever things are of good report; if there be any virtue, and if there be any praise, think on these things."

If your thoughts are not aligned with Philippians 4:8, they do not represent the character of God and should not be trusted. God wants us to acknowledge, accept and have the mind of Christ.

Here is God's love revealed to us through this powerful scripture.

Jeremiah 29:11 "For I know the thoughts that I think toward you, saith the LORD, thoughts of peace and not of evil, to give you an expected end."

As God's thoughts were to the children of Israel and us today, this is the expected end to give us all hope and a future.

The negative thoughts that draw you away from God to doubt His existence and love are only powerful when you choose to believe them. All thoughts are powerful through belief and choice.

Every action a person takes comes from their thoughts, so it is essential to use that power wisely.

2

TWO SOURCES OF THOUGHT

Thoughts are believed to be formed by activity in the neurons in the brain. Scientists have been trying hard to find where thoughts originate within the brain. *Dr. Fred Luskin at Stanford University* says, "the average person has over 60,000 thoughts daily." He said, "of those 60,000[1], 90 percent of them are repetitive through the day and from previous days."

"That's amazing. Our thoughts are a mixture of positive, negative, fearful, guilty, happy, angry, kind...you get the picture. The Good News is that it's totally normal."

Growing up, I didn't understand the origin of thoughts, but I didn't believe they just appeared out of nowhere. It is important to realize that thoughts do not originate with us; they are spiritual in origin and come from God and satan.

---

[1] https://www.yourtimetogrow.com A thought is a thought - yourtimetogrow.com -.

Keeping this in mind, we will explore our two sources of thought.

God is the First Source

In the Bible, God is described as the Creator of all things and the loving Father of humanity.

We are made in the Image of God, and since He is a spiritual being, our thoughts are also spiritual.

God created us as spiritual beings, and everything about us is spiritual. Our spirit enables us to connect spiritually to God's Spirit, through whom we experience the life of God flowing through us.

God speaks through many channels; the mind is one way. God is love, and everything from the mind of God is introduced through love.

God speaks to us through our thoughts in such an inspiring, thought-provoking, encouraging, stirring positive way that we are drawn to Him. So while He may not stand before you to speak, He will help you hear Him through your thoughts and feelings.

Throughout the Bible, God takes the initiative, not waiting for us to approach Him because He desires a relationship more intimate than our needs and desires. God continues to communicate with us today through His Spirit, the Bible, His people, or however He chooses.

During everyone's existence, God establishes a relationship with each individual so that we can get to know and love Him personally. Everyone is unique and different, so He deals with each one based on individuality. As He initiates relationships with us by revealing Himself, our faith responds to the *light* of His self-revelation.

Thoughts that come from God are life-giving and always peaceful. His plans are never difficult to hear for our lives because they come from a place of peace. That is because God is *life,* and His plans towards you are designed to build you up *and* never to tear you down.

Many of us grow up in a traditional way believing when things go wrong in our lives, it's easier to blame God.

It is something I have heard all my life. If not God, who then should be blamed?

Since individuals make wrong decisions, they cause problems for everyone, not God. God has given us His ideas to build on, create and bring everything good we need to live a prosperous life.

In studying the Bible, you will learn to hear God's voice clearly, enabling you to understand that He speaks to us constantly.

God knows our thoughts because He is all-knowing *"(Omniscient)."* Therefore, He does not control our thoughts but leads us to make wise decisions if we follow His lead.

Despite our sometimes-wrong choices, God still allows us a right to choose. Although He knows what you will decide, it is you who will make the decision.

It is essential to understand that God is not hidden. It is crucial to remember this truth because nothing is hidden from God. On the contrary, He awaits our move since He has already moved in our direction.

Remember, the next time you experience peace through thought, it's God speaking through your thoughts to you.

Likewise, we should also be able to experience the same peace when we think of Him.

Untrained ears and spiritual blindness prevent us from sensing His presence in our thoughts, knowing His draw, and hearing His voice. Instead, we hear His voice understand His thoughts and the drawing by His Spirit through a relationship.

The more time we spend intimately with God and His Word, the easier it is to recognize God and His leadership in our lives.

We should see what the Bible says when we have a question about a topic or a decision.

God will never leave us or act contrary to what He has taught in His Word (Titus 1:2–paraphrased).

In addition, we can learn how to recognize God by comparing what we hear with the truth of scripture.

Isaiah 55:8 says, "For my thoughts are not your thoughts, neither are your ways my ways, saith the LORD."

The thoughts of God are infinite beyond our ability to understand them naturally. In the natural, they make no sense to us, but in the spiritual, we can rest in the knowledge that He is good because everything He does is good.

The capacity to forgive, love, be patient, and be kind is a God-given quality that transcends our natural mindsets. Hence, why in the Bible, God spoke in a straightforward everyday narrative to meet us at our natural human level of understanding.

We are left to trust Him, who has all knowledge, to reveal what He *knows* is necessary. He is a good Father, although we don't know everything He plans. There would be no need to rely on Him if we knew everything.

Our parents, for example, may not explain why they tell us not to do certain things while telling us to do other things. However, parents and children love each other, so trust is mutual.

Trust is the same with God; everyone must adopt this attitude, regardless of what they are going through, and our faith will increase in this development.

The more we become aware of our limitations, the more we will want only His thoughts and His will in our daily lives.

According to Luke 24:13-16—paraphrased, Jesus was with the two disciples on the road to Emmaus, but they didn't recognize Him. They didn't recognize Him at first because their eyes weren't opened until they broke bread with Him, then their eyes were opened.

We are all born spiritually blind while hearing the truth but unable to see what it means to our lives. This is because the veil of unbelief keeps our eyes closed.

Is it possible to walk through life and completely ignore all of God's signs and signals? As a result, His appearance may not come in the form you expect.

There is nothing more powerful than faith when opening your eyes to a realm beyond your five senses. The core of our being is God, who is in our thoughts and is the most intimate part of us.

There was only one spiritual being to which we were supposed to be connected: God the Father and the Father through the Son.

Second Source

Satan, also known as the devil, the adversary, and other names that depict him as an evil and crafty spirit, is our second source of thought.

He is a created spiritual being who became evil, roaming around earth diligently seeking followers geared toward advancing his evil agenda.

While thinking he can truly end worshiping God, satan acts irrationally and seems solely infected with the desire to be against God and His people. By any means necessary, he looks to steal worship from God to be given to him.

Since satan is intelligent and crafty, we have not always been able to discern his connection with our thoughts. So, rather than offering a solution, he cunningly lays out something (a thought, an idea) for consideration as bait to lure us into doing what we should not do.

Romans 7:19-20-KJV "For the good that I would I do not: but the evil which I would not, that I do. Now if I do that I would not, it is no more I that do it, but sin that dwelleth in me."

1 Peter 5:8 "Be sober, be vigilant; because your adversary the devil, as a roaring lion, walketh about, seeking whom he may devour."

Satan is described throughout the Bible as arrogant, proud, powerful, cruel, fierce, deceitful, and subtle. To put it another way, he is the core of evil.

When a person enters a department store ready to kill and cause unnecessary harm, do you think the first conceived idea was from the enemy? Even the thought of lying, stealing, and cheating on a spouse came from the adversary's mind.

Sinning against God, which in its simplest form is failure to do what is right, is defined in the Bible. Additionally, sin breaks the law, hurts others, causes violence against others, and is unloving towards others, all of which rebel against God's laws. The Bible teaches that sin involves a condition of the heart, which is corrupted and inclined toward evil, but it is a conscious decision.

The enemy will try to seduce you into sinning against God because he must accuse us of being guilty instead of himself. Although this may sound like something from a science fiction movie, satan is a supernatural spiritual being, but the difference is that he chose to be eternally evil.

We can choose between good and evil, worship God or satan and choose heaven, but satan does not have that choice.

The world is filled with all kinds of evil thoughts satan started, which people execute. There are countless examples of satan's evil villain thoughts being adapted as theme plots in movies, songs, and everywhere.

Whenever your thoughts are filled with guilt, condemnation, fear, confusion, anger, doubt, and so on, these thoughts represent satan's characteristics, personality, and nature.

Ephesians 2:2—paraphrased, says, "he is the ruler of the kingdom of the air, the spirit who is now at work in those who are disobedient."

God is the only one who knows our thoughts, but satan and his demons have been observing and tempting the human race since the *Garden of Eden.* Therefore, he and his demons can observe our words, actions, and reactions; he is an *assiduous foe.* They have learned through many years of experience to make educated guesses and take advantage of our thinking. So, besides being the expert in lies, satan must suggest ideas to get you to respond.

In satan's eyes, we serve as his mouthpiece, hands, and feet to conduct his evil plans. Satan uses us as a tool to steal our blessings, destroy everything we own, and then kill us, as recorded in

John 10:10 "The thief cometh not, but for to steal, and to kill, and to destroy: I am come that they might have life, and that they might have it more abundantly."

So you see, satan accuses us, brings up all our sins and shortcomings, and tells us we do not deserve anything good.

He offers a compelling case against us because he is so anti-human. With a grudge against God, he is fighting to blind humanity from the truth of who we are and can be in Christ.

So, those negative thoughts, feelings of low self-esteem, and depression, which seem to come out of nowhere, are from satan. To detect his lies, we must know the Bible to shield ourselves from his deception, as recorded in:

Ephesians 6:11-1 "Put on the whole armour of God, that ye may be able to stand against the wiles of the devil. For we wrestle not against flesh and blood, but against principalities, against powers, against the rulers of the darkness of this world, against spiritual wickedness in high places. Wherefore take unto you the whole armour of God, that ye may be able to withstand in the evil day, and having done all, to stand. Stand therefore, having your loins girt about with truth, and having on the breastplate of righteousness; and your feet shod with the preparation of the gospel of peace; above all, taking the shield of faith, wherewith ye shall be able to quench all the fiery darts of the wicked. And take the helmet of salvation, and the sword of the Spirit, which is the word of God: praying always with all prayer and supplication in the Spirit, and watching thereunto with all perseverance and supplication for all saints."

Recorded in [James 4:7]—paraphrased, we are commanded to submit to God before we are told to resist the devil so he will flee from us. If you don't know Jesus, you are no match for satan's thoughts.

Regardless of where you are on your journey, surrendering your life to Christ, being renewed in your mind, and knowing who you are as a child of God will help you overcome the power of satan.

Our enemy would like us to embrace religion over the truth of a relationship with God and produce a form of *godliness* while denying God's power. Therefore, even if signs and wonders follow, you must ensure that any thought or idea conforms to God's written Word.

Satan aims to introduce doubt into our minds, so we will reject what we have read or heard about who we are through Christ and the power that belongs to us.

In [Matthew 13:3-7]—paraphrased, the one on whom seed was sown beside the road when anyone hears the word of the kingdom and does not understand it, the evil one comes and snatches away what has been sown in his heart.

In [Acts 5:3], "But Peter said, Ananias, why hath satan filled thine heart to lie to the Holy Ghost, and to keep back part of the price of the land?" Satan put a thought in Anania's mind to lie, and because of Anania's choice to allow that wrong thought, he paid the price of his death.

In ^{Genesis 3:1}–paraphrased, Eve in the *Garden of Eden* doubted God's words because satan got into her head. So, likewise, satan wants non-believers to reject God and what God has said in His Word before they receive revelation. The goal of satan is to control your entire life through your thoughts.

3

WHO TOLD YOU?

After Adam and Eve ate from the tree of the knowledge of good and evil, their spiritual acuteness was immediately enlightened, and they knew what they did was wrong.

God called out to them and asked, "Who told you?" God knew the source but wanted them to acknowledge their role by listening to an unfamiliar voice. Adam and Eve knew God's voice and knew that voice wasn't from God; instead, they hid from God's voice when they heard it for fear of shame.

The same is true today; we would hide from God and avoid the only one who can help us.

After listening to satan's lies, Adam and Eve learned overwhelming shame and insecurities. Satan convinced them through a thought that is always contrary to God and why the blame game was messy. Since no one accepted responsibility, God sentenced them all because Adam blamed the woman, and Eve pointed the finger at satan, the counterfeiter, in the form of a serpent.

The truth is that satan is a bad counterfeiter of God, but as pure evil, he is the enemy who lives among us. Whatever is valuable is more likely to be counterfeited. That explains why everything of value has a fake or counterfeit version, such as Rolex watches and Gucci handbags. The same is true in the spiritual realm; by understanding this, we can see satan's fake nature in the Bible and society.

Throughout the *New Testament,* Jesus spoke in parables to help humanity understand spiritual things. His use of parables combined a spiritual message with a simple narrative.

Here is an illustration that combines a straightforward narrative with a spiritual message.

"Several years ago, we hired a gardener to care for our lawn. The first day he walked around our property, he discovered some weeds that looked like grass in a few spots. He called it crabgrass, the proper name for this weed that grows with and resembles grass. Because we were unaware of its presence, these crabgrasses grew with our grass for years unnoticed by us.

When we examined the weed grass closely, we could see the difference because we were given guidelines for what to look for. Our gardener said the best way to eliminate crabgrass is by uprooting and removing them by force.

Upon discovering the counterfeiter, we decided to stop the crabgrass from continuing to have them infested while growing and destroying the look of our lawn.

We did what our gardener said and pulled the upper part of the grass, then completely removed all aspects of the plant's root with a weeding tool."

In the same way, the enemy satan deceives us with lies that are a counterfeit version of the truth. By finding the counterfeiter, you will identify the source of the enemy's lies.

We have highlighted a few lies you should not fall victim to and the truth you can use instead.

1. The Lord does not want to hear from you after you have ignored Him for so long.

   Truth - God always wants to hear from you, even if it's been a while.

2. My past defines me, and God doesn't want me.

   Truth - No one is too dirty or sinful that God can't forgive.

3. It doesn't matter what you do because God loves you.

   Truth - God loves you; however, what you do matters to Him and us. The Bible gives clear directions about how we should behave.

4. I have tried to fit in but I don't feel I am enough.

   Truth - With Jesus as our atonement, we always have a path back to God. You are more than enough through Jesus.

5. I am the only one who struggles with_____ (fill in the blank).

   Truth - The Bible says there is no temptation that is not common to men. Jesus understands because He took on humanity.

6. God is not good because there is suffering.

   Truth - It is not God's fault; sin causes suffering, and our decisions affect someone else.

7. I desire to be married.

   Truth - Marriage isn't the goal; a deeper relationship with God through Jesus is. Love God first so He can guide you to a spouse.

8. The Bible isn't relevant today.

    Truth - read the Bible, and see if it might apply to other parts of your life. You'll be surprised by how relevant it is.

Here is another Scenario

I heard of a lady at a grocery store who received change from the cashier when one of the bills caught her attention. Although the green color was a little lighter than the other, she noticed the image didn't look sharp, and the paper felt different. It was a counterfeit! The cashier exchanged it for a genuine bill.

The cashier then turned the counterfeit bill to the store manager. I wondered how long it was in circulation and how many people did not notice it and were fooled. She knew to compare the bill against the real thing and focused on the differences instead of the similarities. This is how you can tell it is a counterfeit. You will notice satan's mistakes as readily as a trained eye begins to see the difference between genuine and fake currency through being in a relationship with God and understanding how he works by studying scriptures to gain knowledge about him. The more information and knowledge you have on the enemy will help you identify the differences to expose satan and resist his lies more effectively.

As our enemy tries to influence us through thought, he wants us to be blinded to the fact that he is the one doing it. This is why he restricts your access to the truth through lies, deception, and manipulation that he knows will work on that individual.

We must identify the sender to determine whose voice is being heard and if it is the voice of truth.

The Bible says, "And ye shall know the truth, and the truth shall make you free." **John 8:32**.

The scripture verse also refers to what is consistent with God's mind, will, character, and being. It is, therefore, God's self-expression since truth flows from God.

The moral of both illustrations is what action you will take after discovering the counterfeit and knowing the truth as you journey through life. Why? Because there is an enemy amongst us, he is acting as an angel of light, a counterfeit in our daily mundane lives to hide his true identity. So think about who told you and if it sounds like God or the enemy.

Perception

Like a three-year-old who needs an answer, the mind always searches for answers. Providing an acceptable response is all that matters to a child. Unfortunately, having more information and knowledge at their age makes it not nearly as easy for teens and adults to reason.

The idea has been put forth that people need a reason (purpose), something for their souls, or an answer for areas they don't understand, and when that is achieved, neither God nor His Spirit isn't needed.

It is the human spirit or soul of a person who is neither tangible nor physical but affects the physical body in a way that requires more attention. So in that regard, we would better cater to our spiritual nature rather than our physical senses.

Our cognitive understanding is based on reasoning, intellect, and thoughts as interpreted through our senses.

Did you know your perception dictates what you do with your senses?

As we live our daily and spiritual lives, we use our five senses to understand and perceive the world. As in the natural world, you cannot see air or wind, but neither can exist without the other. Therefore, to better understand your spiritual connection, you should study the Bible and pray and worship God.

This sounds very relational as we will see the world through the Father's eyes and follow the path He desires.

Psalms 34:8-paraphrased. David invites us "to taste and see the Lord is good." David is telling us to put it to the test and experience God's goodness for ourselves. Then, when we spend time with Him, we can hear God's voice clearly over the enemy's lies.

Through our sense of touch and feel, we express gratitude to someone or, in this case, to God. We can feel God's desire and intent in our hearts and know the direction He wants us to go.

Something is always going on in the unseen realm, and God gives us the power to discern it. The understanding that knowledge comes from God, not just the mind, is to realize that He is involved in every conscious intellectual activity we have. With this knowledge, we perceive Him as needing to exist within our thoughts and minds for guidance.

Likewise, what is spiritual is manifested in the natural intellect, emotions, feelings, etc. When done well, the purpose of emotions and feelings is to bring us to a place of communication with others and motivate us to action. Your emotions significantly influence your decisions, from what you decide for breakfast to having a dog as a pet. The fact is, feelings are internal signals that exist, like the red in a red traffic light.

Since we are guided by the character of God and our will, this is not something we need to be reminded of; it is ingrained within us as a part of our existence.

If you were on a plane or climbing a mountain, the altitude changes only if you ascend upward higher. Similarly, we can ascend to a deeper relationship with Him as believers by spending more time alone with God in His presence and reading His Word.

We must listen to God when we communicate and not only speak without hearing what He has to say.

Despite being in heaven, His Spirit dwells with us on earth when we seek to know Him intimately and by obeying Him. As a result, our spirit becomes more aware of Him and sensitive to His presence. We can only understand God's nature through our spiritual vision, not our natural and earthly vision.

We don't just visit Him for encouragement and inspiration; we are to live in God's presence daily. His presence goes before us, clearing the way for us to acknowledge Him in the details of our lives.

We can take control of our decisions without becoming victims of what we see and hear through our senses.

Whenever you enter God's presence, you receive the power to make the right decisions supernaturally because you know who you are and what's suitable for you.

God wanted a family, so He created us not as enslaved people but with the freedom to reason with our intellect. It doesn't matter whether you acknowledge Him. His Spirit guides and directs regardless of whether there is a relationship with Him.

Did you wonder how that person, who we will call Jim, helped you find your dream job and knew when to meet you in the restaurant on the right day and time? You were divinely set up because God's goodness, mercy, and grace of God wanted you to succeed.

Identifying God in your life has never been easier when you spend more time with Him. I am referring to a relationship with someone who enjoys your company, as a relationship with a father to his child, or as a best friend.

Consider this, through faith, we receive God's promises, but what stood out about the heroes of faith is that they were not victims of their thoughts because they believed without wisdom. Our faith should be supported by a revelation, a clear word from God that tells us what to do, but not foolish faith. By faith, a woman gave her rent money to a local assembly believing that God would return it to her before it was due, but God never said that. Later, she said it was an emotional response in the heat of the moment why she lost her apartment. Although she meant well, whose voice was she hearing?

Similarly, the enemy will use our thoughts to interpret what he desires in our senses. Either we will resemble the nature of God our Father or the nature of satan, who is evil.

Do you believe satan exists and exists in your head? Of course, but, on the other hand, we tend to overlook our predator, satan, regardless of what we call him. This is because we are constantly being persuaded or pursued by him. Why? Because we live in the natural realm on earth where he exists and reigns.

It is our responsibility to control the enemy's effect on us. To contain the devil, we must submit to God to resist him. The scripture says he is looking for another opportunity to return after he flees.

We must train our minds, feelings, emotions, and hearts against our enemy as we coexist with him on earth and in our thoughts.

Whose perception are we following? Is it God? With the knowledge that your true self is worth embracing and that you are loved beyond any experience here on earth. Who do you identify with?

Society says if you are a victim of your thoughts, you are hiding in fear of failure and that life won't turn out as you expect. All of us are sinners only saved by the grace of God, but like any gift, we must receive this gift of grace through Jesus' redemptive blood.

From a religious perspective, we are condemned, saved through works, serving others and God, but when religion fails, God says come to Him all weary with a heavy heart, and He will give you rest.

Jesus was not a part of any religion; He was submitted to God, doing whatever God told Him to do.

We are to be followers of Christ and submit to God, meaning to yield ourselves over to the authority of the all-knowing God to direct our lives.

Through Jesus, we are already redeemed, no longer condemned, and free to live an abundant life in Jesus.

We are no longer victims of self-serving shepherds and pastors who are led by false doctrines rather than the Spirit of God.

In the absence of God's truth, the enemy will try to make us lose our identity through lies that we are unloved, through shame and guilt, saying we aren't enough.

If you repent and accept Jesus as your Savior, the Bible says, you are a new creature, all your sins have been forgiven, and you are free to start anew through Jesus, and that's the Truth.

Through Christ, God has already provided for humanity because He knew we would mess up. After all, our bodies see life through perception sanctioning a victim mentality.

4

HISTORY ALTERED FUTURE

W e will look at several examples in the Bible where people have fallen victim to their thoughts due to doubt, fear, or pride.

Throughout the old and new testaments, you will find out how their choices in history have affected their future for the worse. You will also see how it has affected others both then and now.

We will begin with the fallen angel in the **Old Testament**:

Isaiah 14:12-16 "How you are fallen from heaven, O shining star, son of the morning! You have been thrown down to the earth, you who destroyed the nations of the world. For you said to yourself, 'I will ascend to heaven and set my throne above God's stars. I will preside on the mountain of the gods far away in the north. I will climb to the highest heavens and be like the Most High.' Instead, you will be brought down to the place of the dead, down to its lowest depths. Everyone there will stare at you and ask, 'Can this be the one who shook the earth and made the kingdoms of the world tremble'?"

Lucifer, or satan, as commonly known, was the first created being to seek the glory and honor that belonged solely to God. However, instead of being satisfied with his already glorious position, satan planned to rule over God and sit on God's throne to rule the world.

With this scheme of thought, he convinced a third of the heavenly host to join him. Then, in response to satan's evil thought plan, God banished him and the rebellious angels from heaven because of satan's selfish pride. Therefore, demons are counterfeit angels or these banished angels.

Before he became corrupt, Lucifer was named "Morning Star" and later given the name satan, our "adversary," in recognition of his new evil nature. Sin originated in heaven and began in the heart of Lucifer, an angel created by God with superhuman moral and spiritual strength.

As God's enemy and the enemy of all humanity, he tries to control our thinking and discredit everything God created on earth.

As the prince of the air, he roams the earth deceiving humankind, replacing God's thoughts with his counterfeit thoughts.

In the Bible, God has already condemned satan to burn in hell along with all the fallen angels and all who do not accept Jesus as their Savior. If you are not intentional, conscious, and aware, you *can* be taken in by satan's lies.

When we embrace the authority of Jesus, we discover who we are and whose we are, thereby fully identifying our value. In our relationship with Jesus, we are secure in our identity, and the adversary cannot deceive us unless we intentionally entertain and tolerate him.

His use of power for evil altered the course of his life, the lives of angels, and the lives of the entire human race.

Adam and Eve

Satan, our adversary, has continued to rebel against God to include humanity beginning with Eve in the Garden of Eden.

Genesis 3:1-7-KJV "Now the serpent was more subtil than any beast of the field which the LORD God had made. And he said unto the woman, Yea, hath God said, Ye shall not eat of every tree of the garden? And the woman said unto the serpent, We may eat of the fruit of the trees of the garden: but of the fruit of the tree which is in the midst of the garden, God hath said, Ye shall not eat of it, neither shall ye touch it, lest ye die. And the serpent said unto the woman, Ye shall not surely die: for God doth know that in the day ye eat thereof, then your eyes shall be opened, and ye shall be as gods, knowing good and evil. And when the woman saw that the tree was good for food, and that it was pleasant to the eyes, and a tree to be desired to make one wise, she took of the fruit thereof, and did eat, and gave also unto her husband with her; and he did eat. And the eyes of them both were opened, and they knew that they were naked; and they sewed fig leaves together, and made themselves aprons."

It was satan's idea to cleverly enter a conversation with Eve to challenge what God said and call God a liar by contradicting Him. In truth, today, we are tempted to turn away from God because of questions about God's character imposed upon us by satan, the accuser.

How did sin come into the human race? First, it went into the Garden of Eden. Next, it began in the heart of Eve and then in the heart of Adam. Since they were created in the image of God, they were, in theory, temptation-proof.

They were a pure and blessed couple, and when God looked at them, He saw a perfect image of Himself. They would never be influenced by a talking serpent or defy the glorious and loving Father.

In the Garden of Eden, in the heart of spotless purity that God had created, the serpent began to talk to Eve, asking her a direct question, and within minutes both she and her husband's resistance were broken. Sin started to exist in our world and our hearts.

How could it have happened?

Certainly, it was not because of God, for "He is the Rock, His works are perfect, and all His ways are just. A faithful God who does no wrong, upright and just is He. (Deut. 32:4-NIV).

There was something so convincing about the serpent that left her with thoughts about God's character.

Is God telling the truth?

Should I believe what He says?

Do I know better?

I want to choose my path.

Does God love us?

These questions led Adam and Eve further down the path of doubt and disobedience, separating them from God.

The visual desire for the fruit and the twisting of God's Word from satan became so powerful their personal goal led them to the temptation to see for themselves.

The critical point is that the serpent's strategy was not entirely a lie. Instead, the deception he perpetrated was built on half-truths about God's intentions and restrictions. He uses this to manipulate those who choose to listen to his lies.

Please don't listen to his lies when you know the truth.

Adam and Eve did not instantly die physically after eating a fruit from the Tree of the Knowledge of Good and Evil. However, they did die spiritually and later physically because of their decision. The intent was for Adam and Eve and humanity to live forever in a relationship with God and never die. But because of their disobedience, humanity must be redeemed to God through Christ, our Saviour, and cannot live forever on earth.

Aging is an inevitable result placed on humanity because they disobeyed God.

Adam and Eve decided to invite satan to attack humanity with mental attacks at a person's discretion. The reason satan can reign on earth is that they have sanctioned it, and anyone who listens to his lies has allowed it to happen.

By eating, they both opened the door for humanity to choose between God and satan. To choose between good over evil or what is bad over what's good.

Adam and Eve were banished from the garden to prevent access to the tree of life and humanity from living forever in a sinful state. Adam and Eve only knew God and everything good; there was no choice between good and evil, as evil was not a part of their existence.

Is it possible to claim that the enemy tricked them because they did not understand evil, so he cheated them out of ignorance?

Being in a relationship with God should have caused satan's conversation with Adam and Eve to sound strange and unfamiliar. So why did they not ask God what this new voice was?

It's important to note the enemy did not have the power to sway their thoughts; that power was in their ability to choose.

Abraham and Sarah

Abraham and Sarah's only son, Isaac, was the promise of God to the Jewish people.

Genesis 17:15–16 "Then God said to Abraham, "Regarding Sarai, your wife—her name will no longer be Sarai. From now on her name will be Sarah. And I will bless her and give you a son from her! Yes, I will bless her richly, and she will become the mother of many nations. Kings of nations will be among her descendants.""

After years of waiting and believing it impossible to have a son in their old age, Abraham and Sarah began to doubt God. Did their thinking affect their belief that God would keep what looked like an impossible promise? Finally, Sarah was tired of waiting, so she gave Hagar to Abraham so he could have the son she could not have.

No matter how unlikely it may seem from a human perspective, the Lord keeps His promises. God had not only promised Abraham a great nation but specifically that the nation would come through Sarah regardless of her age.

Under the Old Testament, very few barren women had high expectations of bringing children into the world, such as Isaac. Isaac was a type of Christ; through his seed, God had promised everyone on earth to receive the blessing of redemption through Christ.

I think this should grab your attention! Regardless of our religion, ethnicity, nationality, place of residence, social status, or language, we are recipients, not just Abraham.

As Abraham and Sarah did, do not let doubt shake your faith and help a God who doesn't need our assistance. But, unfortunately, Abraham and Sarah, through impatience, became victims of their own choice. The world became victims of their plot since Ishmael was not the promised child. Ishmael is the father of the Arab nation, and they continue to be at war with Israel to this day over first-born privileges.

Zechariah

Zechariah is so important that Luke begins with him when writing about Jesus' life. According to the book of Luke, the Jews trace their ancestry back to one of Jacob's twelve sons. Zechariah is from the tribe of Levi, the same tribe as Moses, Aaron, Abraham, and Jacob.

I love this because it speaks of Zechariah as the uncle of Jesus and the father to John the Baptist. The Levi's are the priests in the family, so Jesus coming from this tribe and becoming the high priest for all of us fulfills the prophecy.

Luke 1:11-14 "And there appeared unto him an angel of the Lord standing on the right side of the altar of incense. And when Zacharias saw him, he was troubled, and fear fell upon him. But the angel said unto him, Fear not, Zacharias: for thy prayer is heard; and thy wife Elisabeth shall bear thee a son, and thou shalt call his name John. And thou shalt have joy and gladness; and many shall rejoice at his birth."

Luke 1:18-20 "And Zacharias said unto the angel, Whereby shall I know this? For I am an old man, and my wife well stricken in years. And the angel answering said unto him, I am Gabriel, that stand in the presence of God; and am sent to speak unto thee, and to shew thee these glad tidings. And, behold, thou shalt be dumb, and not able to speak, until the day that these things shall be performed, because thou believest not my words, which shall be fulfilled in their season."

Luke 1:36-41 "And, behold, thy cousin Elisabeth, she hath also conceived a son in her old age: and this is the sixth month with her, who was called barren. For with God nothing shall be impossible. And Mary said, Behold the handmaid of the Lord; be it unto me according to thy word. And the angel departed from her. And Mary arose in those days, and went into the hill country with haste, into a city of Juda; And entered into the house of Zacharias, and saluted Elisabeth. And it came to pass, that, when Elisabeth heard the salutation of Mary, the babe leaped in her womb; and Elisabeth was filled with the Holy Ghost:."

Luke 1:57 "Now Elisabeth's full time came that she should be delivered; and she brought forth a son."

Luke 1:59-60 "And it came to pass, that on the eighth day they came to circumcise the child; and they called him Zacharias, after the name of his father. And his mother answered and said, Not so; but he shall be called John."

Luke 1:62-64 "And they made signs to his father, how he would have him called. And he asked for a writing table, and wrote, saying, His name is John. And they marvelled all. And his mouth was opened immediately, and his tongue loosed, and he spake, and praised God."

Zacharias was dumb to prevent him from spreading doubt that would hinder God's plan. Nevertheless, Zachariah didn't lose the promise; he just couldn't enjoy the process of speech. God's promise of Zacharias having a son named John would be fulfilled in God's time.

A prophet is needed to herald the coming of the Messiah. Otherwise, Old Testament prophecies are not fulfilled. Likewise, the prediction about the Messiah's first coming is not fulfilled if one or more of the prophecies is unfulfilled.

Zacharias's son, John the Baptist, was the prophet who announced Jesus as the Messiah. Without God's intervention, Zacharias's unbelief could have changed the outcome of this situation and life as we know it.

His incapacity to speak about his son's pending birth was a price Zachariah paid because of his doubt that the good news was too good to be true. Unfortunately, doubt has persisted since the beginning of time and continues to hinder our enjoyment of life. Do not fall victim to doubt.

Judas

Judas Iscariot is the disciple who betrayed Jesus, as recorded in Mark 3:19. He is known for being a traitor who is dishonest, deceitful, two-faced, and untrustworthy enough to betray a friend.

Even if you have not read the Bible, you have heard something about Judas's legacy. Judas indeed allowed himself to be deceived by satan's thoughts. However, Judas knew he had a choice; he had a choice to be loyal, so why did he depart from it? Judas had a secret sin and took this opportunity in exchange for his greed for money to betray Christ.

This opportunity presents itself to all of us, also called doing what is wrong for our selfish gain. As a result of Judas' stealing from the disciples' money bag, satan gained access to him and instructed him to continue to commit these crimes.

Could Judas have done anything differently to prevent satan from entering, or did he have a chance to avoid it? John 13:27 speaks about satan entering Judas. So the answer is Judas opened the door for satan to enter his heart.

Judas shouldn't have come into agreement with satan's thoughts. But, when Judas listened to satan's lies, he did what no one should have done. While God forgives confessed sins, unconfessed sins multiply to fester more sins, giving satan a firmer grip on our lives.

Judas may have failed to understand the consequences of his decision and subsequent actions of betrayal. Tormented by his thoughts, he desperately tried to return the money and ask the authorities to release Jesus. Ultimately, his thoughts led to wrong decisions and actions that led to his death.

It is important to note that sin (not doing right) after it has taken its course; if you do not accept the redemptive power of Christ, the result is death. God's power shields you from the guilt of sin, shame, disobedience, and the power of evil.

It's recorded in all four gospels that Judas concealed his sin and, therefore, could not prosper due to satan's guilt and shame imposed upon him, but had he renounced them, he would have experienced mercy.

In the Bible, we are urged to learn from the scriptures that everything written in the past was written to teach us so that through the endurance taught in the scriptures and the encouragement they provide, we might have hope. I paraphrased this scripture, but it is worth reading in Romans 15:4.

We have supplied scripture verses demonstrating how those who tolerated satan's ideas and thoughts suffered greatly. If we allow satan's ideas, we will repeat history's mistakes of living in fear, doubt, and pride rather than in abundance and embracing God's plan to give us hope and a future.

5

IT'S YOUR CHOICE

In this chapter, we will examine your thoughts from a choice-making perspective rather than just an innocent victim's perspective. In life, it is all about choices. We make choices all the time, although most choices are just reactions.

You may decide that a prime rib steak dinner is the best idea to cover feelings and thoughts when you are hungry, sad, and stressed. The best way to decide is by knowing what your goals are. You can make better choices by knowing what you want out of life.

You have a choice, so take your time, think about how you want to respond, and consider what is right, all while loving yourself and treating others with compassion and love.

What is an excellent choice?

An excellent choice means you're heading in the right direction, using the right strategy to correct the problem; you make the best choice based on what is proper.

We often avoid some excellent opportunities because we are afraid of how they will feel, even though they'll likely be better than we think.

Bad choices, on the other hand, end up being counterproductive and can quickly begin spiraling into stress, confusion, and despair.

Our choice is primarily dependent on our value. Your value or worth is based on what God said you are through the redemptive blood of Jesus.

I read about a researcher who assessed how people would feel if they won or lost money and how they felt when they found out they had won or lost.

People naturally turn their expectations of value into feelings. Therefore, it is unclear if people would maximize their gains and minimize losses if they focused on their feelings or objective values. We become victims when we do not listen to our emotions and go with our feelings.

For example, we do not always need an emotional reaction to sadness, such as crying. Instead, we need our emotions to guide us to what is important in life as a value judgment.

While decision-making is the process that leads to action, critical thinking is the element that defines the choice as sound. God gives us a free choice to live our lives as we want. The gift of choice is that no one can force you to decide.

A refusal to listen to God will put us in apologetic situations unwillingly.

God wants us to make our decisions within the blueprint of His will because we love Him and desire to obey Him.

God created you wonderfully, but we live in a world where if we allow the influences of our culture and society, it will produce selfish people with little value in human life.

In the same way, you cannot avoid making mistakes because you're human. There are erasers on the end of pencils because people make mistakes. What you can avoid is making the same mistake more than once.

How information is presented can affect the decisions we make as a whole. The people who deliver it know this and may capitalize on it. When you fail to hear important information, think incorrectly, or do not understand fully, you can be a victim of your thinking.

With that said, I wanted a pickup truck without monthly payments a few years ago. I felt I deserved a new truck but thought I would settle for certified used. Buying a used truck for cash seemed like a good idea because I thought I could fix any problems this well-maintained vehicle may have. Unfortunately, after two years, I could not fix some of the repairs, and for six months, the repairs were like monthly payments.

Ultimately, the truck that initially passed all electrical and mechanical tests cost me mentally, physically, and financially. Having spent much money repairing the truck, I purchased a new SUV. During my final purchase negotiations, I was blessed with a discounted price which enabled me to keep the truck.

One Saturday afternoon, my truck was parked in our driveway when a young man driving by saw the truck and stopped. The young man asked my son, standing outside, "is this truck for sale?" There wasn't a for sale sign on the truck. But, the young man said he wanted to purchase my truck because of the make and model to start his lawn service business.

Since I was uncertain if I wanted to sell, I told my son to tell him I was firm on a specific price. However, while I was now willing to sell the truck, the young man wanted to pay less. At first, I wasn't ready to comply, but the young man's persistence paid off, and this young 19-year-old entrepreneur returned two weeks later with the exact cash amount I wanted.

I learned from my truck experience that we can become victims of our thinking if we don't listen to the right voice. Unfortunately, I felt victimized by my own thoughts that day as I shared my frustration with my wife. However, my choices and decisions were based on my own free will. Ultimately, we either listen to or follow satan's proposals or God's leading.

Relationship

How we think also influences how we interact with others and ourselves. We were made for relationships.

God established from creation, and in His Word, that man was not meant to be alone. Therefore, He gave Adam a suitable partner for a wife. As Adam contemplated God's creation of Eve, He thought: Wow, how wise of God, then Adam called her Woman.

Essentially, this is where humanity started and the first clue that satan had entered our thoughts and was establishing his spiritual relationship with humanity.

Satan, the serpent in the Garden of Eden, suggested a subtle relationship between Eve and Adam. Their choice to accept without careful consideration landed them in a relationship they were not expecting nor created to have.

The connection we have with God teaches us how to have healthy relationships. Conversely, when a relationship with God is not established, satan can intrude and taint it with his ideas of relationship. Satan does not want you to have an intimate relationship with Jesus nor understand your spiritual life through the redemptive Christ. Instead, satan wants you to move through life according to his system when you don't have a relationship with God. His strategy of ignorance is not good because you think you are doing life and being yourself.

Whether or not to be ignorant through your life journey is a choice. As Jesus accesses God's spirit for us, ignorance is not bliss because you will worry and be in harm's way about what you do not know

Suppose, for instance, you stay in an abusive relationship believing they will change without any evidence supporting this claim. Satan has convinced you that you deserve it, but you should not listen to what he says. Instead, you must reject thoughts of a relationship that is abusive and toxic; this is the enemy and not God's purpose for your life.

However, any relationship that doesn't have the rock with the principles of God will not be prosperous and are not from God's thoughts or His mind.

What is imperative is your significance to God, that you should be more conscious of Him than of sin.

You are precious to God, and He wants to emphasize that to you.

Forgiveness Is a Choice

In recent years, church hurt has been a topic of discussion in the Christian community.

This is when the enemy takes advantage of offenses in the local assembly by causing discouragement, frustration, and, the biggest, unforgiveness.

Church hurt refers to the disappointment we feel when someone in our local assembly or the Christian community does not live up to some level of our expectations. While you may think that your expectations were not met for a good reason, remember that people are fallible, everyone has a will, and everyone is not on the same level as you.

When we rely too much on leadership or another viewpoint without understanding the Bible clearly, it is easy to become a victim. It is important to note that people hold onto their pain and brokenness and that we must also discern leadership by God's Spirit for their pain and brokenness.

The enemy will suggest inappropriate behavior, a thought to offend another, or to act negatively toward an individual, a local assembly, a religious institution, or God.

New believers may become victimized if they don't know who they are and cannot differentiate the spirit from their flesh. In addition, because they lack boundaries and are not honest with themselves, they are vulnerable to the enemy's lies.

We must choose to allow the Spirit of God to transform us daily into the nature and character of God. Unfortunately, everyone that attends service is not Christian, and some are borderline believers. The church consists of believers, not the building, and Jesus is the author and finisher of our faith, not human beings. I can also judge your actions concerning scripture as I judge myself similarly.

Unforgiveness, whether you are a believer or not, is like stabbing someone; instead of that person feeling pain, you feel it yourself.

Forgiveness is a personal choice and an action verb commanded by God, which signifies spiritual maturity and a love characteristic of God.

Seek God's will, and He will place you in a local assembly where you can grow. The most important thing is to forgive everyone, regardless of whether you believe they did wrong or acted appropriately. It's not that person; it's satan using him or her against you.

Ever wonder why you are sometimes happy and sad because you - can choose whether to continue that thought and its emotions?

For example:

What you think - I have been betrayed;

What you feel - I feel sad, mad, and hurt; and

What you say - I feel betrayed.

Here is what you accurately feel - I feel sad because I think I have been betrayed.

Feel your disappointment, then release forgiveness towards the person who has disappointed you.

In truth, we are called to live in harmony with each other and all of creation, except satan, who must be rejected.

Choosing whether you want to place your standard high enough to do the right thing or sufficiently low to negotiate self-gain as the enemy would be best.

The grace of God cannot be extended to another if you do not know that God has extended grace to you. Can we still be hurt as believers without forgiveness and claim to be followers of God when we understand forgiveness and choice? Humanity has the CHOICE to love and forgive within and outside their local communities, regardless of whether we are Christians. We are to live by the standards of the Bible and not be influenced by cultural or religious influences or any of satan's lies.

God gave us all a choice to receive His love freely, and then we freely give to everyone.

Here are some practical ideas to consider with a personal choice:

Do not let stress get the best of you when feeling stressed out and anxious when facing a tough choice.

Do not rely on mental shortcuts that speed up our ability to make judgments but can be biased.

Do not be too optimistic and overconfident in your abilities to make good things happen.

Take that good advice you would give to a friend you care about.

Ask a friend that has been through the same dilemma.

Reframing the information you received can help you to choose.

Remember to give yourself some time to think it through.

It is hard to think clearly under pressure; when you face a difficult choice, let it come to you.

Instead, walk away and do something distracting.

Play a game, read a book, chat with a friend.

It is my goal, just as it should be yours, to make the right decision the first time around. It is not a mistake to repeat the same mistake twice; it is a deliberate act.

New creations in Christ have a newborn spirit and access to an omnipotent Savior greater than all the world has to offer. Even though they love God, satan can tempt them to sin because they have a choice and a will.

The concept defies logic and explanation, but isn't it true that most people think sin is most understandable for Christians? Why? Because we all commit it.

Remember how John starts the second chapter of his letter: [1 John 2] "My dear children, I write this to you so that you will not sin." This letter's author encourages believers to stay in Christ, in His thoughts, and not let the enemy influence their choices. It is written for us so that we will not sin; [Genesis 39:9] "How then could I do such a wicked thing and sin against God?".

We should vow not to facilitate the lies of satan with our will instead of being shocked at another sin.

Like Eve, she could have said, God, this serpent is trying to trick me, but she wanted to listen. They were intrigued to hear you will not die, but your eyes will open, and you will have knowledge of good and evil as the gods do. Then she realized it was good to eat and desirable to make her wise; I believe she took the risk of being curious about what could happen.

It was listening to satan that planted the seed of doubt, which led to disobedience. In a materialistic world, we prioritize our physical needs first. Our thoughts are limited and earthly and on the here and now. We miss what God is trying to show us since His thoughts are always on the big picture. His are unlimited and unsearchable.

During your thought process, determine what is inspired by God before choosing a direction to follow. The only thing God wants from us is an open heart to do His will.

By weighing the pros and cons and seeking godly counsel, we can make a good choice if we have an open heart, pray, meditate, study scripture, consider the circumstances, and consider both options. Then, God can easily guide you when you are still, listening, and willing to accept guidance.

Every person has the power to choose and follow God's plan for their lives through the power of choice

An Audience of One (You)

Ultimately, it is never about people, competitors, or spectators; it's about you as the audience. Why? Because you decide on which thoughts to think about. We are more than just observers or listeners in our daily lives.

Although the thoughts, words, and actions of others can influence us, our minds are soaked up with information from all directions, whether it comes from TV, social media, family, or friends.

One person always stands out at any event, and spectators wait in anticipation to see what they can do. But, of course, we want someone to shoot the ball in the basket and win the game, dominate the show, and control the meeting. So, you are the person to win the basketball game by shooting the ball before the end of the game.

It is your thoughts and decision to manage a successful show and organize that meeting well. You are the audience, not a spectator; your thoughts and choices determine your life's outcome.

You are the one who is responsible for your decisions and actions, not the person who had the idea or inspired it. Similarly, passion and lust will corrupt your mind if you do not control them.

We tend to set our standards for what constitutes a victim. But, unfortunately, this standard is based on lies that claim we did not understand the ramifications of our actions and decisions and did not consider the impact on others. Where do you think that thought was formed?

My definition of a desired thought is what you want, your decision, and your will over everything else. I define a real thought as one God intended for you to follow, but sometimes you don't.

God's attempt to fulfill your destiny is in your real thoughts.

His plan is much more wonderful than our desired thought if only we can consider His direction.

Every one of us must control our desired thoughts over our real thoughts. While we may look like spectators, we continue to play a game that we are lousy at without self-fulfillment. We usually use these kinds of explanations to support our justifications.

To make ourselves look good, we place ourselves as victims in our poorly played game started by satan. We say that omitted information misled our beliefs by leading us to misbelieve.

We have all experienced situations in which information was withheld or presented, but we decided to trust or act anyway. Being preoccupied with the many audiences that surround us daily isn't normal.

For example, an individual's mindset varies according to cultural beliefs. Decode your cultural beliefs according to the Bible; the Bible is the blueprint for what is right and wrong.

Judge if your culture and standard of living are moral, then you decide if you are an innocent victim of the thoughts you were taught to believe. Your past experiences influence the thoughts you have today.

Satan's primary source to fuel thoughts is through our hurts or unresolved issues we carry from our past. The toxic thoughts you have today may be from a series of minor incidents that were not correctly managed, and it isn't necessarily from a traumatic childhood experience.

As a result of improper processing of these thoughts, they become negative emotions and feelings, producing harmful matters of the heart. Your mood can change negatively by just an idea, which means satan is at work using your past experiences.

When your mood changes from good to bad, this is God's doing, but either way, it is up to you to choose.

Ecclesiastes 3:11 states God has "set eternity in the human heart." This proves humans are different from other forms of life.

We instinctively know there is more to life than what we can see and experience in the here and now, and we know there is something beyond. Although you cannot fully control the thoughts that enter your head, you can manage and rule them once they have entered.

6

DESIGN PATTERN

Your design pattern is influenced by how well you see yourself, or lack thereof. A habit or a particular behavior that individuals have when they repeatedly enjoy something good or bad. It is up to each person to decide whether to indulge in those habits or behavioral patterns.

The root of a good habit lies in good thoughts, while bad habits derive from unresolved issues in our lives and practicing bad thought habits.

Another way to put it is that your brain receives a good or bad thought, marks it, and interprets it as a standard to be replicated if you continue to accept it.

We can break the pattern of poor habits if we acknowledge them initially, such as overspending, smoking, cursing, and alcoholism are a few examples.

To avoid their dominance, we must manage our thoughts carefully. So let's pause for a moment to think about how you see yourself.

The problem may be that you are listening too long to satan's negative and evil thoughts about yourself until you have become it. If only you could see yourself as God sees you, as created to reflect Him by ruling over satan and every negative thought. The Word of God is so personal that even you can find a personal God to transform your life.

A negative pattern is difficult to ignore when it develops due to emotions such as lust, sadness, unforgiveness, unhappiness, or whatever the negative thoughts might be. However, if you allow negative thoughts to dominate your space, these thoughts will run your life.

Whatever healthy thoughts you allow in, like eating healthy, reading the Bible, listening to worship music, or something beneficial you enjoy to dominate your thoughts, will be helpful. Instead, when we see you, we know that seed that is unhealthy, hurting, wounded, in guilt and shame to diminish your influence will destroy your destiny.

If you are humble, God is near and willing to hear, but you must choose. It is all about your decision to intentionally seize your thoughts to determine the pattern it takes since your design is an individual habit that is characteristic only to you.

God created you, but you have the choice to be the creator; you customize and choose a design behavior choice into your life. We are all designers of our lives through our thoughts by letting good and not unhealthy habits dominate our lives.

God designs our thoughts (usually good); however, our thoughts (usually evil) are suggested by satan or altered through satan's suggestions.

We have become accustomed to an unhappy pattern because we failed to pay attention to our thoughts. My parents had taught me **boundaries** when I was a child, which I took very seriously. So, you might be thinking, **boundaries**, what is that?

I define boundaries as limits you set by saying "**NO**" to create a healthy sense of personal space.

Being prayerfully aware of your triggers, regardless of whether you are a believer. In an attempt to get you out of **God's** boundaries and the boundaries you have set for yourself, the enemy sets a trap for you.

What's the reason? Because he (the devil) does not want you to be free. The devil uses many plans to restrain us and prevent us from growing based on what he has watched us respond to. His evil plan aims to keep you from becoming all God created you to be and carrying out all **God** has called you to do.

The devil wants you frustrated, so indirectly, he is helping you frustrate yourself through thoughts. The enemy's goal is to cause us to violate our **boundaries** through guilt, discouragement, and lies. You don't want a pattern of being a people teaser struggling to tell others how you feel because you lack **boundaries**.

In addition to guiding your heart, you should also set **boundaries** for your emotions, time, and energy.

It is vital to set up clear **boundaries** with others, follow up with those **boundaries**, and not let others manipulate you are some ways you can avoid becoming a victim.

When you have established some **boundaries**, take a well-ordered look at your weaknesses, as they may cause you to step outside them.

Look at past mistakes that made you make inappropriate decisions or behave unwisely. Do not put yourself in a situation where you know you will face temptation; identify them, and then say, with God's help, "I will overcome them."

With **boundaries** implemented, your life will become much more peaceful, less emotionally draining, and better for protecting our mental health.

Like a cross stitch pattern, an unprofitable behavior pattern can be learned quickly without realizing how dangerous it is. Your negative pattern choice will only get worse with consistency. As a result, people are unreliable, liars, abusers, murderers, or exhibit other negative behavior patterns.

Your destructive thinking will harm your family, circle, community, society, and the world as a whole.

When you want to break free from negative habits, you must work hard and be dedicated to the process.

First, you must recognize you are in a pattern or a cycle.

What are your negative, destructive patterns?

Be accountable by taking responsibility and checking your emotions.

Identify the causes and be honest with yourself.

Take a different choice of action by getting the help that you need.

Be kind to yourself and see yourself free.

1 Corinthians 10:13 "The temptations in your life are no different from what others experience. And God is faithful. He will not allow the temptation to be more than you can stand. When you are tempted, he will show you a way out so that you can endure."

The longer you think about something that doesn't serve you well, the more tempted you are to do it.

Your passion may have vanished, and you are unsure of your life purpose. But God is calling you to return to Himself, repair your mistakes, and enjoy life again.

Whatever you are struggling with, you can have hope in God, come to Him, and accept His plan for success.

Isaiah 53:6 "All of us, like sheep, have strayed away. We have left God's paths to follow our own. Yet the LORD laid on him the sins of us all."

John 10:11 "I am the good shepherd. The good shepherd sacrifices his life for the sheep."

Sheep are similar to humans in many ways, including being timid and prey to enemies while relying on their shepherd for survival. However, sheep are remarkable creatures like humans because they can recognize the voice of their shepherd even when they are gullible.

While it is true that we choose to stray by satisfying our desires, like sheep, humans can also hear the voice of truth if they want.

We can cultivate our relationship with God and listen to Him like sheep following their shepherd.

For every dysfunction, habit, or negative pattern you can be healed of, God has laid upon Christ the sins of the whole world.

When John the Baptist saw Jesus, he shouted, "Look! the Lamb of God, who takes away the sin of the world!" John 1:29.

Listening to the enemy's lies led the children of Israel into captivity, so we must remember that if we don't follow God, we will also become victims.

In the Bible, God compares people to sheep because He views humanity as valuable and priceless.

Be open to God's plan for your life and commit to the process of becoming the person you were created to Become.

7

THOUGHTS ON TRIAL

W e will look at your thoughts to evaluate them in a court of law. An individual is on trial for the intention or premeditated thought they had that led them to commit murder, cause a car accident, receive a traffic ticket, etc.

If you allow negative thought patterns to accumulate in your mind, you may have to admit that you are a victim of low self-esteem, improper thoughts, and lies and deception.

During the Seventeenth Century, crime victims were initially recognized as victims to justify the need for a criminal justice system.[2] However, victims then and now are still stereotyped as innocent.

---

[2] A victim of crime did not exist until well into the 17th century. Why were victims ignored for so long? A victim is an integral part of the system; some say that without a victim, there would be no need for the CJ system. www.criminal-justice.iresearchnet.com/forensic-psychology/victim-participation

Some say no one is genuinely innocent since humans are prone to making mistakes. However, in most cultures, people believe one has to do something wrong or sinful to earn or contribute to their destiny. But of course, if you want to blame a victim, you will find something to place the blame on them.

Likewise, we tend to blame abuse, rape, and assault based on our perception instead of who is at fault. Therefore, you are not at fault, even if you believe you did something wrong to cause the attack.

Instead, the attacker's wrong mindset and bad behavior led to the attack. Unfortunately, in my experience, when speaking with a victim or a victim of abuse, they usually are the first to blame themselves.

Being identified as a victim is problematic because it is a heavy burden and can be challenging to prove. In addition, victims carry the shame of betrayal, being in the wrong place at the wrong time, or having the memory of what happened to them.

To prove your innocence, it is up to you to supply evidence like in a court of law; you are presumed innocent until proven guilty. Therefore, the first step in building an innocence defense is ensuring you are innocent. Even if you think you are innocent, you may have broken a law you didn't know.

The enemy likes to set up traps to accuse us without us knowing. Satan does not need anything to accuse us of; his goal is to bring your mistakes or weakness into the picture so that you will doubt or be afraid because of his advice.

You will need an experienced defense attorney who can examine your charges to ascertain your chances of conviction. Then, your attorney can build a case around your innocence if you're not.

Throughout the years of watching a plethora of crime mysteries, I learned that you don't have to prove your innocence to avoid a conviction; if you have not committed a crime, you would have to prevent the prosecutor from proving your guilt through premeditation. What is more effective is to expose flaws in the prosecutor's case than to build a complete innocence defense. However, there is still a risk of conviction, and you will need to fight for your freedom by any means necessary.

You can start by gathering information by evaluating its causes and effects and admitting your fault or inexperience. Then, when you assess the data collected, you can also decide if your thinking was flawed.

Nevertheless, you cannot say your beliefs were wrong stemming from ignorance, a lack of concern for the outcome, or the desire to fulfill a self-gratifying need. However, in this trial, you will not need witnesses, phone records, employment documentation, financial information, photos, videos, DNA, etc.

Jesus represents those who have trusted Him before God's throne of grace. 1 Timothy 2:5 "For, There is one God and one Mediator who can reconcile God and humanity—the man Christ Jesus." He died in place of humanity to reconcile humans to God. Romans 5:10. "For since our friendship with God was restored by the death of his Son while we were still his enemies, we will certainly be saved through the life of his Son."

I recently learned about *Cognitive Behavioral Therapy* (CBT) and the *Dialectical Behavior Therapy* (DBT) approach that involves CBT.

CBT is a therapeutic method that changes automatic negative thought patterns. It helps with identifying negative thoughts and reframing them into more balanced thoughts.

The pandemic has caused a lot of stress. At least this concept will help reduce depression and anxiety since our thoughts can influence our mood.

I will touch on the overview of putting your thoughts on a trial involving testing the evidence of thinking. It is done with a comprehensive workbook or a therapist; you can initiate the process of analyzing your thoughts.

It works as you focus on examining irrational thoughts, taking a negative thought to court to determine whether or not it is fair to think that way. You will act as a defense attorney, prosecutor, and judge as you compare evidence for and against a single thought.

In a real court of law, only verifiable facts are permissible as evidence. Any opinions, assumptions, and conjectures are not allowed.

Try this exercise with the thought of being unhappy, and record your results.

First, you will identify

Facts:

Sticking with the facts, identify the situation that has generated a strong feeling.

Where and when it happened, who was involved, and what happened?

Identify the Moods:

Describe any emotions associated with the situation, including positive and negative ones.

Identify Automatic Thoughts:

List any immediate thoughts that come to mind when remembering the situation.

Gather Evidence:

Identify evidence that supports the automatic negative thought and does not help the thought.

Evidence Supporting Thought:

Evidence Not Supporting Thought:

Our thoughts are not always facts; we can change how they affect our moods by examining and changing them.

Participating in the thought trial exercise is valuable since it allows you to consider your thoughts from multiple perspectives reasonably and logically.

Since you are doing this alone, have an impartial friend or counselor who can help you by challenging evidence that you think breaks the rules and presenting evidence you missed.

I hope this benefits you as a way to put your thoughts on trial.

In John 8, Jesus provides defense against the adversary's accusations brought by the scribes and Pharisees.

The following is a Biblical scenario in which a woman is accused of adultery without being required to prove her innocence and instead used as a victim of satan's scheme.

God judges us through Christ's sacrifice and atones for our sins, whereas we all are victims. Jesus is the master defense attorney; there are no juries because there is no need for a trial.

Lastly, the no-name adulterous woman represents the expression of God's love and redemption in Jesus.

This story involves the scribes and Pharisees looking for anything to trap Jesus into saying something to use against Him; they brought a woman caught in the very act of adultery to him. They threw her in the middle in full view of everyone expecting Jesus to be responsible for condemning and participating in stoning her to death.

They wanted to remind Jesus that the *Mosaic Law* demanded that she be stoned to death. However, the law required both participants to be stoned. Where is the man?

By trapping Jesus with this woman, they only wanted to exploit Him by not bringing the man to Jesus. They asked Jesus what His thoughts were on this *Mosaic Law* on the punishment of this adulterous woman.

Jesus stooped down, started writing something in the dirt, and said, "if any one of you is without sin, let him be the first to throw a stone at her." One by one, the people left, leaving Jesus and the woman alone. Jesus said to the woman, "where are your accusers?" She answered, "there are none' and Jesus said, "neither do I accuse you; go and sin no more."

John 8:1-11 Jesus returned to the Mount of Olives, but early the next morning he was back again at the Temple. A crowd soon gathered, and he sat down and taught them. As he was speaking, the teachers of religious law and the Pharisees brought a woman who had been caught in the act of adultery. They put her in front of the crowd. "Teacher," they said to Jesus, "this woman was caught in the act of adultery. The law of Moses says to stone her. What do you say?" They were trying to trap him into saying something they could use against him, but Jesus stooped down and wrote in the dust with his finger. They kept demanding an answer, so he stood up again and said, "All right, but let the one who has never sinned throw the first stone!" Then he stooped down again and wrote in the dust. When the accusers heard this, they slipped away one by one, beginning with the oldest, until only Jesus was left in the middle of the crowd with the woman. Then Jesus stood up again and said to the woman, "Where are your accusers? Didn't even one of them condemn you?" "No, Lord," she said. And Jesus said, "Neither do I. Go and sin no more."

Jesus addresses the woman as a representative of us being forgiven for any charges, accusations, wrong thoughts, and bad decisions. Through unconditional forgiveness, we can enter a relationship with Jesus. Based on this relationship, Jesus has challenged her to sin no more, no longer be the victim, not deceived, but to live for Him.

She as we can find our identity in being a child of God. He silenced the critics while healing her heart, which was burdened with guilt and shame. Jesus skillfully highlighted that no one is without sin and the importance of compassion and forgiveness.

God sent His only son Jesus into this world to save us from the condemnation we rightly deserved.

The scribes and Pharisees left thinking like victims tricked by the one they tried to deceive.

God's love is evident in the forgiveness of our thoughts that led to negative behaviors.

8

INTENTIONALITY

Since you are defined by your decisions, let's explore how our thoughts can guide you in making the right choices. The problem with making decisions about our lives is that we are involved in them. This means we have a vested interest in the process and the outcome, making it difficult to play the victim role.

The process involves being intentional with how you think. No skill is more valuable and more complicated than the ability to think about problems critically.

Schools do not teach you a method of thinking; you must do your due diligence. But on the other hand, being intentional can keep us from becoming victims.

The *Ten Commandments* have principles regarding both our relationship with God and our relationship with others. God established the *Ten Commandments* in the Bible, which are at the core of society's laws. Are we acting like rebellious people instead of following the rule of the *Ten Commandments?*

How we react to something depends on what convinced us that the decision was correct. As long as we embrace Jesus as our savior and allow Him to work through us, we can protect ourselves from wrong choices and being victims of our thoughts.

Spend time reading God's Word and praying (talking, being in a relationship) with Him daily.

It is the Word of God that the *Holy Spirit* uses to renew our minds and thoughts. Therefore, take the time to study the Bible for clarity and not just read the Bible as a religious ritual. Spend time to reverence God in worship, listen, then intentionally obey Him with action.

When you commit your life to the LORD, you must grow in Him intimately and through His Spirit. Every moment you have, spend time with the LORD, meditating on His Word, and praying. God's Word reveals His will for your life. You will develop an intimate relationship with Christ as you do these things, keeping Him at the center of everything you do. Your life will begin to change as you walk with Christ and have communion with the *Holy Spirit*; you will do all things according to biblical principles rather than rely on human wisdom. Upon realizing God's gifts for your life, you will begin to analyze motives and desires in light of God's ultimate purpose.

Fighting against evil thoughts and developing spiritual discernment to have good thoughts is essential.

The *Old Testament* defines obedience as *"listening"* or *"hearing."* It is a hearing with reverence to obey, as in the *New Testament,* it implies *"hearing under"* or *"submitting oneself to."*

Learning how to transform your thoughts will change the entire course of your life. Remember that God put a hedge of protection around Job to protect him from satan, as in (Job 1:9-10).[3]

Therefore, we should ask God to put a hedge around us to protect us from satan and ourselves.

Romans 12:2-KJV "And be not conformed to this world: but be ye transformed by the renewing of your mind, that ye may prove what is that good, and acceptable, and perfect, will of God."

Also, put on the whole armor of God. Read Ephesians 6:13-18.

If you're finding it difficult to control your thoughts, try googling scriptures on controlling your thoughts and recite those scriptures daily.

James 4:7-NIV "Submit yourselves, then, to God. Resist the devil, and he will flee from you."

Knowing who you are in Christ means renewing your mind and thoughts through the scriptures. So here are a few of my personal mantras.

- Memorize scriptures by placing them on an index card, sticky notes on a bathroom mirror, a wall, or a note section on your phone.

---

[3] Satan replied to the LORD, "Yes, but Job has good reason to fear God. [10] You have always put a wall of protection around him and his home and his property. You have made him prosper in everything he does. Look how rich he is!

- Use your authority as a believer by memorizing, knowing the scriptures then standing on them.

- Refuse to think thoughts you know are not going to produce faith, hope, love, or promote holiness.

- Surround yourself with people who promote goodness in your life.

It is understood that everyone does not have the same mindset; therefore, choose your friends wisely.

- People with different mindsets will influence your thoughts and negatively affect your decision-making.

- A practical thing to do is to avoid negative thoughts such as; "there is no point in trying" or "nothing always works out for me."

- When you say, "everyone thinks I'm boring or strange."

- Don't predict the worst by saying it's not going to work.

- Don't be a mind reader by making assumptions about other people's thoughts.

Here are ideas to get rid of negative thoughts:

- Observe your negative thoughts and self-talk.

- Reflect by journaling and exploring your inaccurate beliefs.

Question them and make changes; for example, you're probably not incompetent or stupid.

- Create statements that realistically counter your negative thoughts and self-talk.

- Practice mindfulness by being present at the moment and aware of where you are and what you are doing.

- For inspiration, listen to motivated teachings that encourage building up your mind

- Journal - write down what comes to mind or how you feel daily; it will help you release frustration and anger.

Just putting thoughts on paper will clear your mind and decrease stress levels. In addition, this will help you understand what is happening inside you before you talk with a trusted friend, family member, or therapist for help.

To overcome toxic thoughts, you may want to consider.

Be kind to yourself; do not let negative thoughts rule you; instead, like King David in the Bible, "encourage yourself."

1 Samuel 30:6 KJV And David was greatly distressed; for the people spake of stoning him, because the soul of all the people was grieved, every man for his sons and for his daughters: "*but David encouraged himself in the LORD his God.*"

Self-talk is that private conversation we have in our heads around the clock. Then, when our inner voice is determined to be heard, we say what we think aloud. Sometimes, our internal chat takes the form of a review of our communication with others.

In our verbal interactions, we tend to evaluate what we said after the fact, often criticizing ourselves for not saying what was really on our minds, for example:

- What you wanted to say was no, sorry, I am unavailable.

- Instead of agreeing, I should have said, you will need to find someone else.

Our lives are filled with silent conversations in our minds, enabling us to understand ourselves and those around us better.

There is a guiding voice that tries to convert the subtle differences between our perception of physical reality and what we experience within it. Therefore, it is important that we consider the messages we send ourselves and that we look for underlying lessons to take away from them.

- The real point is knowing when it's time to take control and stand up for yourself.

When your priorities are being talked down by what gives you an excuse to cheat, ignore your goals, or be irresponsible, it may be a sign your inner voice(*the enemy within*) is trying to trick you into making a decision that is contrary to what you have already decided.

- You can gain new perspectives and insights if you step outside yourself and stand as a neutral observer.

- Stopping improper or negative thoughts is taking control of your thoughts before they control you. Then with a clear head, address what you are thinking.

- Discovering that small quiet voice within (God) creates a sense of peace and harmony. By learning to hear that Voice, we can discern the sound.

- When Love is within, the Creator can reveal it to you when He speaks.

- If it is not worth thinking about, do not continue with it.

Depending on your level of self–control, you may have to repeat this until you get your thoughts under control.

- Do not stay stuck another day!

- It is essential that we can dominate our enemy in real-time and not in reverse, as he is under our feet for us to rule over.

You can be intentional about disciplining your thinking by doing a few or all these things.

I heard someone say, "repetition is the mother of memory," so the more you practice by being intentional and disciplined daily will bring about good results.

- Daily discipline is the key to your success in making better decisions.

9

VICTIM NO MORE

By relying on God and being in His Presence; you can overcome any negative thought, struggle, or challenge. It is said whatever you care about, you will fight for. Your thought life is valuable and worth fighting for. With that said, you are already on your way to success!

In no way should a victim's mentality be tolerated or blame and excuse be inserted. Do not be swayed by what you think is right; do what is right only by knowing which source is drawing you. Since everyone can choose between good and evil, this will not be easy.

Our minds and bodies battle dominion daily between good and evil. When the enemy has your head, he has your mind, which means his lies will lead your thoughts and heart.

You cannot trust your head or heart after the enemy has led you into brokenness, hurt, and shame. The *Good News* is that God can restore your life to fulfillment while healing your wrong mindset, heart, and all the pains that come with life.

We are here to help you see yourself so the next generation won't be compelled to fix what you couldn't while trying to live their lives. Therefore, you must avoid succumbing to a wrong mindset and becoming a victim of your thoughts.

There is no way to overstate how important it is to submit to God, guard one's heart, and obey God if one wants to escape satan's trap. Unfortunately, we have no authority to come against the powers of darkness in our strength. We go against them in the Name of Jesus; it is His Authority, not ours. Remember whose authority it is in which we operate.

To obtain the things God has promised us in His Word, we must be willing to fight until we receive them.

Do not become the victim of your hurt by not releasing it; give God your guilt, shame, or unhappiness to Jesus for healing.

In the end, God is the only one whose opinion matters. His love results from who He is, not what you do. No matter what others say about you, your identity in Christ stays the same.

It is my honor to speak into your life to empower you to own your thoughts. To unlock your full potential, you must permit yourself and take ownership of your life. Unfortunately, many people entrust their lives to others or even become prison guards themselves. They forget that they have the key to unlocking the full potential of their lives.

I am here to remind you it is time that you permit yourself permission to live in abundance in every area of your life.

God is calling you to own your dominion, receive your rights, and be free from depression, guilt, shame, and anything that hinders you from being the person you know you can be.

Permitting yourself to succeed is the first key.

Do not give in to those thoughts that you cannot succeed.

You can accomplish great things by not being afraid of success.

The misconception is that success is achieving a lot of money or being greedy.

You must rid your mind and body of such mental programming since it is a lie from satan.

The definition of success depends on you and your acquired knowledge of how to get there.

Your idea of success might be being a good parent or spouse, exercising before 7:00 a.m., or taking small steps toward your goals.

No matter what success means, you must own it and live up to it!

Please write your own definition of success and move towards it, not what society says success is.

Set more behavior-based goals instead of outcome-based goals to make success a habit.

To lose weight, make the right food choices instead of defining success based on the number on your scale.

The outcome will follow if you keep succeeding at the behavior-based goals and move in the right direction.

You may have a strong desire to start that business, write that book, start that non-profit, or become a first-time homeowner.

These are good God ideas to fulfill your purpose and success in obtaining exemplary accomplishments correctly.

Satan's job is to trigger fear, doubt, and low self-esteem to discourage you from doing anything good.

Recognize these triggers and reject them.

Understanding failure is a form of learning; we should not punish failure.

Failure is not a requirement for success; if anything, it amplifies success.

By making mistakes, you learn and build the character that transforms every other area of your life.

Your mindset changes and you embrace success more because of your effort.

If you let go of the fear of failure, you will be free to explore the possibilities of your life.

Your potential will grow because you realize that mistakes help you learn.

Every media outlet (news, magazines, and social media) shows successful people.

It seems like they are perfect people living flawless lives.

They are people like you and me who have learned from failures.

We are not looking for failure, but if you have failed, know that there is no failure in God because He makes everything beautiful again.

Be yourself by permitting yourself to be yourself while being honest with yourself.

"To be yourself in a world that is constantly trying to make you something else is the greatest accomplishment." — *Ralph Waldo Emerson.*

Trying to live up to the expectations of others can be stressful.

Being yourself will attract the right people into your life, and you won't have to waste energy presenting a fake version of yourself.

The first step to being yourself is to accept yourself, not pretend.

You need to accept your flaws as well as your good parts.

We put on a mask because it is our instinct to get accepted in society.

You can and will survive if you are not part of a group.

God will give you access to so many people; you do not have to fear people's rejection.

You will always find like-minded people if you express yourself as you are with confidence in trusting who you are.

Reject those thoughts of rejection. They are not you; the enemy's suggestion is to keep you down.

Let go of all the emotional baggage.

Forgive yourself and move on with all you have today.

You get to define your future; it can only be great if you stop hurting yourself with the pain of the past.

Get your emotions and feelings together before it becomes a heart issue rather than redirecting your anger, guilt, or shame.

God has given you a sound mind; the enemy wants you unstable.

Your future self is now in your hands.

Define your God-given values, set goals, follow your passion, and stay true to yourself.

Embrace change and change what does not work for you or what God reveals to be wrong for you.

Raise your standards and let go of your past negative identity and change the people around you.

You need to learn to say no to people and experiences that do not appeal to the nature of God already inside of you.

Life is too short not to be genuine.

"I can't give you a sure-fire formula for success, but I can give you a formula for failure: try to please everybody all the time." — *Herbert Bayard Swope.*

Permit yourself to be happy

You deserve to be happy NOW.

You do not need to wait for more money, a vacation, or a spouse to be happy.

We often spend our lives thinking about our future happiness.

It is okay to desire more success, but first, you must learn to be happy with what you have.

In any case, whatever you have in life is because you believe in God.

God plans to change your life if you trust and seek Him.

Do not listen to the enemy's lies!

Mindfulness and gratitude are both helpful in developing happiness.

Take a break and do something you find fun or relaxing.

If you have a bucket list of the life experiences you want to have, seek God's guidance.

These are your thoughts from God but choose to acknowledge Him in those simple planning matters as He desires to give you good results.

Nobody else will permit you to live holy and happily like God.

Psalms 16:11-KJV "Thou wilt shew me the path of life: in thy presence *is* fulness of joy; at thy right hand there are pleasures for evermore."

True happiness is a blessed life that comes from seeking God above all; everything will be given to you.

Another way to be happy is to help others.

Kindness makes the world a better place and lets you see past your life problems.

You forgot to appreciate God's grace and mercy somewhere along your path of desire to please Him.

In creating us, He knew He would never pull away from us when He led us down the right path, but we took the wrong way.

Instead, He is faithful to complete the work He has started within us.

He always reroutes us back to the center of His will as we obey.

Are you afraid to decide about something because you don't want to have regrets?

You have made so many bad decisions that you want to make the right one for a change.

You want to ensure that you get things right with the Lord.

In ^{Matthew 28:18-NIV} Jesus said, "All authority in heaven and on earth has been given to me."

Jesus has promised His Authority to those who are His own through a relationship with the Spirit of God.

The problem is that we do not believe it or exercise it effectively.

You must fight the good fight of faith without wavering, for God is faithful who has promised.

Whether you become a victim or victor, the choice is yours, depending on who you choose to listen to.

The decision is in your corner to choose daily to listen to God and not satan.

Your eyes are the light, your heart the issue of life. If the eyes turn dark, you become victimized by it.

The key is to prove God's voice over the enemy who lays in wait for your soul in a destructive way.

God sees us as individuals capable of persuading any decision to be made at any time based on the goodness of our thoughts.

^{Jude 1:24-KJV} "Now unto him that is able to keep you from falling, and to present you faultless before the presence of his glory with exceeding joy."

Remembering the consequences of tolerating ideas or voices that we failed to recognize as wrong is essential. Moving forward, we will reject any thoughts or suggestions that steer us away from what is right or into what is victimhood.

It is crucial to take the time to absorb the information you read and apply it as wisdom. There are two forces in the world: One enables you to make the right choices, and one leads you to make the wrong choice. Choose the right path so that **You Do Not Become The Victim of Your Thoughts.**

10

ACKNOWLEDGEMENT

All honor and praise to God for the privilege to be vessels that God is using to bring encouragement, insight, and hope to everyone who reads this. Although we are not psychiatrists, our knowledge is based on life experiences, studying scriptures, interaction with people, being in ministry, and in obedience to God.

Our faith does not require us to be indifferent to controlling our thoughts; we are grateful to God for the lessons we have learned due to falling victim to our thoughts.

We are lovers of God committed to living out our faith as believers actively by serving God and His people.

We pray that you will all see Jesus as a friend who walks alongside you at every stage of your life. I pray that you are inspired to encounter

Him through His Word as He reveals Himself so that you may enter into a relationship with Him and be transformed by renewing your mind.